By definition, consecration person to another out of long, abiding love, as a setting apart an aspect of living for higher, spiritual purpose, as commitment to God. The book's epigraph notes, "We walk into that which we cannot see" (Elizabeth Alexander, "Praise Song for the Day"). Thus, consecration is faith in action, "the ocean's mouth muscling open for communion" ("The Consecrations"). Throughout the book, a powerful loveliness and affirmation for things made holy encompasses Kevin Clark's poems. Consider "Two Stories," where a couple "swell up with their own resolve, / survivors of lice-laced coffee grounds, / puddled water," and persist "in the community of marriage" and "become the power of myth." There is no mistaking the allusion to Joseph Campbell; as myths ride the cyclical universe, the one couple's story leaps archetypically to another couple, who, after movies and gelatos, find touch "is the wall / beyond which we may choose not to see." We understand: faith, love, and commitment obliterate walls, and take us to sight beyond sight. Consider, again, "I Want to See." Clark writes, "I'm told all of my yearning is foolish, / Forget what you want. Forget the ghosts," the "long odds," and "gods / Cocooned in their silence." "Forget," he writes, "the best intentions and the worst." Rather, what is sacred and life-giving is "the bowls sunning on the table," "this breath this light / This meal this touch these words." Although we may find ourselves "in the whispering valley" of doubt and "dread permission" for death to come ("The Oscillations"), what arises is resolve against the inevitable:

> by God,
> you're alive right now, this very moment
> widening like a summer day, the mother
> you never had backlit in the park, saying,
> Baby, the world's all yours. Make it count.
> ("Elegy")

Gloriously, poem after poem, Kevin Clark makes it count, and "there's / that sound, a soft blue song / sung through you" ("The Driver").

—Mark Sanders, winner of the Western Heritage Award
author of *Landscapes with Horses*

THE CONSECRATIONS

Kevin Clark

STEPHEN F. AUSTIN STATE UNIVERSITY PRESS

Production Manager: Kimberly Verhines
Cover Art: *Amarylis* by Elaine Spatz-Rabinowitz

IBSN: 978-1-62288-918-1

For more information:
Stephen F. Austin State University Press
P.O. Box 13007 SFA Station
Nacogdoches, Texas 75962
sfapress@sfasu.edu
www.sfasu.edu/sfapress
936-468-1078

Distributed by Texas A&M University Press Consortium
www.tamupress.com

for Amy, as ever

For Laura —

... with great admiration
for your work
and in the singular spirit
of the Garden State ...

Best,
Kevin

1/27/22

We walk into that which we cannot see.

"Praise Song for the Day"
—Elizabeth Alexander

TABLE OF CONTENTS

TWO STORIES

—wire service photo, Hungarian border

Once again the migrants eat the road.
In the paper, a young couple, fit and hungry...
I study them like ancestors. They hug, wave
at the camera, having hung from a raft
then slogged the alien miles before
crossing a demarcation unknown
to the earth upon which it's drawn—
an invisible stripe running on like a joke
that's been told and re-told since the first
line was drawn in the dirt. The couple
swell up with their own resolve,
survivors of lice-laced coffee grounds,
puddled water, grasses in the center lane.
In the community of marriage
they've become the power of myth.

*

At the movies last night I sat next to my wife,
laughed at the sardonic jokes, the wise
American actress, her domestic comedy
asserting its complex of new ethics.
I knew we'd soon walk into the night,
order caramel gelatos, then go home
sloshed in the plush boat of all that cream.
And so, for a few mindless hours, we
entered the same domain the couple
would have entered in their own country
had the joke of history not demanded
a new version of the same moral—
Once inside, our very touch is the wall
beyond which we may choose not to see.

ONE

ADMITTING BELIEF

We were sun-wrecked and itching to go back
from lunch into the green lakewater, when
the lifeguards screeched their whistles over
and over and we looked up to see them waving

everyone out. Calm, fatalistic, Protestant, you
bear with me when I tell this story every few
years, nod, shake your head, tell me, Go on.
My mother demanded we come to her and so we sat,

watched the pool go lifeless while a big woman
screamed and pointed *there* and *there* and again
there at ripples under the high dive until it became
clear her kid was missing. Five decades later I fear

it's true: Someone's always missing. This time
I don't describe for you each scenario I've dreamed
and told too often. One may be right there, around
the corner, or may be hiding, counting seconds

in his room, the shades down, the lights off,
the clock and phone cords pulled from their sockets.
Or another may have taken off in the pitch inhalation
of 2AM so no one will sense her empty bed, or

she may be missing in the altogether breathless
way that surges like adrenaline, the cop on duty
not picking up the phone that hasn't yet rung,
can't ring because the fathers or wives or roommates

can't bring themselves to dial, can't enter the phase
in which to call is to admit belief. Some nights
my trouble is, I can't escape the incoming silence
of alarms that tell me I should believe in something

other than the pulse knifing my temple. After
my mother huddled us onto the blanket
in the branching shadows, I kept waiting for her
to say it was time to pack, head home, we have to go,

now. But she sat, rapt, peering at the ripples
for minute after howling minute. The year before,
as we ate after-school snacks, she'd hung up the phone
too slowly, her face literally gnarling with grief

and rage when she dragged us into the living room,
then made us kneel at the coffee table, the rosary
vibrating in her bloodless hands. You say, for some,
prayer's a comfort, a means. Soon enough,

three lifeguards with thick rope hoisted the body—
its awful white—up the wall where they performed
the useless rituals of respiration. Why did she need
to watch? You take my hand, tell me my mother

was a driven woman, so righteous even god
would think twice before talking back to her.
Tonight she too is among the missing.
I can't shake her last skeletal image when

the screen in the cancer ward flat-lined. Bodies
float to the surface. I squeeze your hand, hold on
to what it is I have. Outside, closing in—the dark,
the wind, the ceaseless, invisible gatherings.

THE OSCILLATIONS

Forget the peaks. It was the valleys
took me down. After the doc slipped
from the room, we leaned against
each other, the little range
of spiking mountains beeping
across the monitor. Every time
I'd descend between each tone
I could hear an elaborating wind,
as if air itself was attempting language.
I'd never seen my brother blanch,
the light smearing our faces
yellow like the dead
November grass. And damn
if the old questions didn't start
clawing up. But I kept them
to myself. My brother doesn't bother
with much doubt. He's got a rosary
in his pocket. I used to own one
too. A devout friend reminds me
that the beads are a gift held to the lips
so the lips know what to say. And
this was our mother
we'd been keeping vigil for,
the last breaths. There must be reams

of scripts plotting out my words—
Moses, old catechisms, Peter Pan, then
Tom Swift and that Wright Brothers book
from the Paramus library, Shane
the novel, then Shane the movie. And
all along, tales of walk-off homers.
And the heroic histories beneath

the Christmas tree. My friend Sherman
prefers books of numbers, says
the stories write themselves
because we can predict everything
but the future. That first night
my mother insisted she was going
to beat this thing. We didn't call bullshit.
All her life she'd ground any problem
into concession. Never let go. The doc
gave her maybe one year. It took four

weeks. She thought she'd failed, both
me *and* herself. Damn your philosophy
professor, she'd said too often. My friend Ralph
sat next to me in class, all Jewish poise.
She loved him despite herself. He'd never
cared if there's a god or not. The prof
tossed off the sentence so matter-of-factly,
declared himself an atheist. And
there it was. The fluorescent light
yellowing upon me like a web of nerves.
There's no knowing. Then there is. Then
we're in the whispering valley.
Once I'd heard my mother worry
to the family priest that just this sort
of *G-D thing would G-D happen, Jews
at a heathen school,* etc. But, hell,
she never knew the worst. Two years later

my mind split in a dark room, mid-
seventies, "All Along the Watchtower"
wiring the air, nothing but stems and seeds
in the bowl, our cash in the wind. Black tee,
jeans, boots, long hair shining black

with road grease, stomach paunched
behind a gun Ralph later guessed
a Smith and Wesson .29. I couldn't
know then the scene was preface.
Could the brute dealer
have been a murderer *and* a cliché?
At twenty I didn't expect the in-your-face need
to accept my own death. The guy coughed
from some hellish bellows, said the money
we'd put up for the pound was stolen,
they'd get the guy, was good
as dead. We waited out the lie.
In his one florid hand an entire book
of matches blossomed sparks
as he sucked from the hookah. Still,
at that moment, even as I tasted
sulfur and puke, the flare rained down
the mountain and I could decode
Vonnegut's line in the smoke, how
we are who we pretend to be. Back
in the hospital the high-frequency light
painted us into speechlessness
as we stared at the end of breath.
Strange what returns. The dude
could have killed me, but shit if he too

wasn't reading some script. Before
the spikes flattened into the swale
of that jaundiced room, my brother
and I tightened our arms around
each other. Is there a parallel world
in which the two of us make the scene
a radiant castle? Outside, we'd grant
the whole family an exotic password,

and, when each had practiced it into prayer,
we'd cross the moat to a fanfare score
celebrating our mother's splendid life. But
in this world, my brother and I walk out

to a waiting room where cousins
and an uncle fall with us into a huddled cry.
A voice leads us in a slow Hail Mary.
I've never told anyone: An hour before
the monitor's long final tone, the form
she'd become gurgled, then arched
for breath. That's when I leaned close,
whispered the dread permission
—vocables I'd no doubt plagiarized.

THE SHAPES AT QUECHEE

Ambulance techs serving me through the double doors

          —and then,

a stepping off the edge, a plummet
of morphine and coumadin

       —like these winter dreams

of the deep gorge into which we peered
at Quechee last summer, the updraft,
the pointless creek beneath, until
a slight surge slowed the fall

         so I might listen

to my wife's airless pause as the nurse asked
for power of attorney.

   *

      Should you both die,
posed the lawyer years before,

       who executes

the trust, who gets the kids? I had once thought
unendurable pain forces us like cowards
to let go. And yet in that law office I soon felt
an old comfort I couldn't place,
as if it were a memory, a dream predictive
of the plush tumbling.

       And when the scare reversed

from mortal *clot* to simple, painful *pneumonia*,
I still couldn't shake the way
I'd slid down that tunnel until I rested,

         buoyant

in a morphine dream. On the ER table
I actually tallied the check-list:
my wife's long touch, the children's muted pitch

at dusk, the poems on my desk, all the friends,
even a few base hits—and finally, of course,
that protective paperwork, when,

                              in the ecstatic clutch
of what I knew right then was merely a drug,

                                        too readily
I thought, okay, if need be,

            *

                    I can give it all up.

That evening we'd sat quietly on the dock
of the summer cottage as the dome of dusk
collapsed in increments and the mirroring surface
of the lake reflected the sharp inscription of pine tops
with diminishing care.
                    It's true: We project this life
as a form, a profile in flux, contoured
by blood and brain.
                    Bare-chested, ten, my son
was still skirting the shore for mussels, while
his younger sister sat in an Adirondack chair behind us,
carefully shaping silhouettes into her sketch book.
As ever, the outline of my life swelled
to their dark, blurring edges
                    —and I looked out
over the last reflections,
                    conscious
of my family's small, mammal movements,
of the shape beyond those shapes I so loved in that moment,
such a thing as I'd never let go,
unaware I'd soon be too horribly content

                              to hold on.

ELEGY

I'll never forget that punk Cagney jabbing words
like shivs as if he knew everything
was black-and-white as the movie. Plump
with urban blarney, his old friend the priest
visits just before his hanging, tells him, Listen,
it's not too late, the ticket to heaven is acting

the coward when you climb the gallows. That way
the street kids won't have a bad guy for a hero.
You think, Well, maybe. —Or maybe going good
is a fool's dream. We all know Cagney was pissed
at the universe for the lonely Jack he was dealt,

how he would have told the orphans the end
is close as tomorrow's gruel, grab
what you can. Then he would have laughed
in their faces. Can you see the thing

forever announcing its arrival, like grey rust
crawling up those silver skyscrapers
every dusk, no matter how good or bad
the deck? Maybe there ain't no heaven,
maybe there is. So what do you do

when the two cops lead you to the last
stairs you'll ever climb. Either way,
you'll be dead in a few seconds. But by god,
you're alive right now, this very moment
widening like a summer day, the mother
you never had backlit in the park, saying,
Baby, the world's all yours. Make it count.

HANK'S CHOICE

Each beer means Hank keeps hold
of his dead wife's hand, as if she's been
sucked into a wind tunnel, his grip
a last hope. Not that Hank would say
such a thing. It's funny, the choice
hope insists on… I've spent a life testing
myself against my father's return. How
would he find me? I'll be reading, then bang
he's back to life. Flesh and breath. Strange
he's no older than the day the aneurism
lit fireworks in his eyes. I'm twenty years
his senior. He's astounded to be here,
can't believe I'm so gray. We peer
at each other with tenderness. He asks me
about the Cardinals, how've they done?
And shit if my voice doesn't break.
That's where it gets dicey, right?
Last night at the cowboy bar after work,
I told Hank about this every-few-months
habit of mine. He couldn't admit to hearing
me, not yet. I figured he was too busy
feeding his wife the life-blood of his grip.
How long before any of us choose to let go?
Hell, my story rarely gets *me* by. I told Hank
how I finally ask my father, What's it like
to die? Funny, his younger voice offers,
no one gets it. You'd think a person drifts
off. But there's a surge, no white light—
It's as if you get to relive one memory, and
the right choice floats you past joy
into permanent calm. My father webs out
the fingers of both hands on the table.

It's like the comics I used to read you
before bed, he says, like a fourth dimension
instilling your final field of vision.
Only you're not *seeing* it, exactly.
This one scene materializes inside
your head, every item assembled
into a perfectly still hologram, all lit
from within. —I must seem a lunatic
to you, he pauses. So I ask, What
did you pick to remember? My father
stares at me as if I were inhabiting
his déjà vu. That's when I looked at Hank
dreaming into his glass, pretending
my voice was drowned by the juke.
I told him sometimes I can startle up
from my book, as if the objects
of the world radiate some kind of belief
in themselves. Is it true, or is my heart
gone soft? Kind of like an old song
you still love, even though its whole point
is the sort of bullshit made to fool you
into feeling better about feeling bad.
Like there's a tin ring to this very story.
A drunk drummer once told me
guys on steel guitar are prone to bend
all sideways, start leaning into heaven
while the rest of the band waits and waits
for the fool to find his way back to plumb.
Here's a stone cold fact, I said: Too often
the moment goes sick, my father's face
tiling, his mouth a hole of silence until
he fractals away, all that sentiment used up
like in the old days when the mescaline
took a bad turn and all you could do is grip

the armrests, trust you'd come down
as true a version of yourself as you'd been.
Hank barely heard me above the howl
of his fifth beer. Leukemia don't need to be
the end, he declared, several patrons
wobbling their heads his way. I gave him
an old look, waiting out the choice
both friends hear before it's spoken.
—Well, too goddamn often it does, I said.
He lifted from the stool, spilled a few dollars.
Said, Cards lost again last night, didn't they?

CONCEIT

When I was a kid, Hitchcock's *The Birds* wrecked
my sleep for months. Sometimes it still does. But
not for the gruesome scar-the-night reasons
you might think. I hated the ending. All those birds

settling in as if they're taking over. Was I simply
supposed to put up with that? Maybe I was fighting
off the future I'd seen in my parents: Arthritis,
pissy arguments, that daily bus from Jersey

to the city. The constants. Then again, maybe I was
in the early stages of contrariety. At twenty-four
I was a union president. My wife still calls me
the Young Turk. Maybe I've got a thing against figures

of authority, all their warnings. Still, I have to say,
in '63…? No way would I have thought *The Birds*
an eco warning. Only Godzilla carried *that* gravitas.
My friends left the theatre, but I refused. No kidding,

I stayed in the balcony of the old Westwood Cinema
waiting for the next half. I figured an intermission
split the story in two. But the quick opening credits
roll and once more Tippi Hedren walks right past

Hitchcock and his two schnauzers. Maybe in my first
inklings of what makes legit art, I thought the ending
was a cop out. Okay, a kid wants closure most,
but that wasn't the all of it. Maybe I'm rewriting

my own memory again. Weren't my parents
a loving couple? Did my friends really leave me?

And come on, No way at thirteen could I have known
that's Hitchcock in his cameo. What is it with me?

Even as I write this, my original conceit is dissolving.
In the pitch dark, I'll often roll over to find my wife
gone. Every time, I forget: she's running before work.
There's no getting back to sleep. There's no end to it—

TWO

MUSEUM OF THE MORNING AFTER

—11/9/16

The elevator aspires
to its usual upswell, but
the rising keens
like a dirge.
On the floor of Ancient Traditions,
the breath
of each canvas sours
my neck.
Before a pen and ink gargoyle,
my eyes
study the disfigurement,
the creature's broken skin
blistered, its extremities
tortured
into horrific
directions. That night,
—bed as statuary—
I can't put back the bones.

BEFORE DINNER

You refuse. But in Gaza, in Madrid. In Boston, in Butte—
they're dying irretrievably, all of them. Something
like my young father thirty-nine years ago in a hospital

in Jersey. Fueled on Jameson's and their gut-sure aversions,
his laughing parish friends improvised eulogies
to keep the devil from our home. In the empty shell

of muscle memory, I shot hoops by the garage, the basket
he'd put up for us, the ball in its downward parabola, like
every person, good or bad. So I prayed then never once

to ask him, even in the waning strength of my prayers,
to return to me. There's no Zen in your refusal. You're
furious I'd think our friend's time is near. For an hour

my old Catholic resignation makes you hate me. It's true,
we agree: Heaven's just a wet dream. Maybe that's why
you can't believe in the calmed breath when the bullet, the last

come-what-may, finds the center. In today's local paper,
20 year old Mike Mitchell in Baghdad is dead of that very
bullet. Soon enough, the choke-throated calls begin. In Miami,

one last bottle kills Julio's mother, in Pittsburgh both Jim
and Sue of cancer, ditto Jake next door. In Chicago
both Miller kids in a crash. When I returned stricken

from the oncologist to tell Aunt Mary that my mother
didn't know she had at the outer limits of any hope
two years to live, Mary said, *Two years is a gift.* More

than the words, her brute calm affirmed the old family
fatalism. One month later, hairless and gagging on chemo,
my mother slowly flat-lined as I held my brother

and stared at the monitor. This second, a fullback
from Donora, PA is flapping his own flesh over leg bone
while his captain scans for snipers. No matter how,

none of us will return. While you purple in anger, never
grief, another friend repeats a mantra in an ancient
tongue. It works for her. Look, I admit, I've never been

Jim, or Sue, or the Mitchell boy. But I've been caught
in my father's last blank look. I've touched my mother's
boiled skin. Like them, we've got no choice. Still, right now

I'm hungry and breathing. Call that abundance or just
getting by. Call it my love for you. It's the reason
I'm thinking you might go out for a walk. I'll wait here,

chop tomatoes, some onions and basil for soup tonight.
When you get back, I'll open wine, we'll eat good bread,
tell stories about every one of them. We'll laugh a little.

THE CALLING

(—the day Sister Bernice decided)

This was the year of our curiosity. Did we have
the calling? Fifth grade and we girls followed
Sister Carmel at lunch like a comet tail
through the parking lot. Puritanical accomplices,

we'd sweep down upon the seventh-grade girls
winding ribbons through each other's hair
under the giant old eucalyptus. *Their door locked,*
darkness spilling like airy ink, like incense

from the thin crack below. Then the sweaty
eighth-grade boys grunting through touch football
on the church field, and the third graders running
from Sister because on a bet they'd taken spice cake

into the yard. *Again last night my mother*
crying out, as if pain didn't hurt. Did we have
the calling? Would we become nuns and live
in perfection as she did with quiet friends

and rosaries behind those darkened third story
windows? *My father calling and calling out*
my mother's name. So we asked about
the private convent chapel and was it true,

the story about Sister Anne's missing finger, and
we asked about the dinners she and the other nuns
ate each night and who got to drive the one car
they owned and why did Mother Superior

speak in such a far-away accent. *Like the hurt*
in his voice when grandfather died in the accident.
And all along Sister Carmel smiled and laughed
and kept on coursing the invisible gold path

I imagined winding out before her like another one
of God's secrets. *Were they praying to each other?*
It sounded as if they were taking turns praying
to each other. And all along she'd give baffling

little oohs and crinkly smiles. Then she'd raise
her eyebrows as if to quiet us, as if to hint
at a single unimaginable detail about which
we'd speculate for endless nights in our rooms

on the phones our parents finally installed. And once,
I couldn't help myself, I asked if she'd ever been
in love. And she laughed as if she were a human bird,
or—I dared to think—as if she were a nun's version

of the Holy Ghost, her trilling so rich with secret
that we all looked at each other and none of us
ever asked again. So rich we never spoke
of the question that entire year. *Why the sudden*

silence, nothing moved in there, that darkness
like pitch black smoke at the door? So rich that
I never told even my best friend Mary Kathleen
what happened later as I was leaving school out

the side door where my mother would be waiting
in the car. Sister Carmel put an arm around me—
her furtive glances down the hall—and she whispered
in my ear, Bernice. Child. You asked if I've ever been

in love. And her voice lifted breathy and nearly
sad, as if ancient sounds in some far-off dream.
Bernice, such a question. Of course. I've always
been in love: I've always slept with Jesus.

DOG

1.

We saw the gun, then froze. It's Berkeley,
we're posed on a ball field, the pitcher
fiddling with the tripod and screaming
in his pot-hazed laugh that we assholes
better huddle tight, when some lunatic friend
of the shortstop's leans loose-kneed
behind the catcher, pulls the chrome long-barrel
from his jacket, waves it skyward, and fires
so loud the pressure knocks us off plumb
'til we scatter in slo-mo backward flight.
Thank God for *those* moments,

                     I'm thinking
two decades later, as Lily's husband Brick
turns from the faux marble kitchen bar
to curl his arm beneath her left breast, then rub
his thumb upward in a slow, half-moon arc.
I'm past forty, ever the romantic. Even
in the blaze of college drugs, sexual show-offs
were like garage rock, the drummer
always off beat. My wife is squeezing my hand
hard beneath the kitchen counter when Brick says,
Show them... And our friend laughs
in that high pitch, third-glass-of-white-wine riff,
No, honey, of course I can't *show* them...
And as her face reads like a lost language,
I'm ready. I'd seen enough absurdist acts
at the psychedelic theater of our youth:
—nothing could throw me now.

2.

There are those rare people born immune
to threat. Either that or they flat-out like it.
Not me. As a young man, my chakra
were fine-tuned to go taut and sing
nervous in the slightest psychotic breeze.
My courage ran to cross-country, each step
past the lactic edge a measure
of just how far I could detach myself
from the immensity of suffering
down there in my legs. But in college
I'd learned to push the high-voltage panic
into the peripheries so that stillness
would pass for calm.
                              I still remember
the night after the guy pulled the gun,
how my skin thrummed
at a sound past hearing when
my girlfriend's brownies lush
with seeds in slow-cooked butter
lured the cop sirens of the flats
over our mattress on the floor.
Sleep as distant tease, I watched
the wailing arc through the window
convert to matter, enflesh
into a cross-legged swami
with lizard head, a duplicity
holding forth two consecrating hands
upon which a swirl of diamond blades
formed and reformed the pre-strike S
of a hooded cobra. For a timeless
ten seconds I faked myself Buddhist,
imagined a future in which my blood pressure
pooled into calm so the reptiles

would dissipate.
                    In a blitzed instant,
we'd been known to paint the night
fluorescent, free dance on bedroom walls.
But this was different—I found a way
out of panic that night by telling myself
how the story would play in the ears
of friends I didn't know yet.

          3.
Once, I recognized some distant twin version
of myself in a magazine. It wasn't me, but
as sorry-assed as I knew that portrait
to be, I couldn't help but read my twin self
cutting edge. I knew the trick to dope
was never turning back to check yourself out
for too long. Otherwise, some animal incubus
could open its eyes to stare back
through the jamboree mirror.
                    Many stories later,
when I began this poem, I actually thought
our Sixties hallucinogenic orbiting-into-the-weird
had been good prep for whatever
sudden freak show splits the cracks
of the quotidian. As if the windowpane
and the good gold and even the white crosses
had fired up so many electric dramas
that the idiosyncratic suburban tremors
to come would seem no more annoying
than the fifty-foot patch of deep sand
I'd plod on my run to the edge of town.
I'd even been nostalgic for the old dialect
when weed glazed any sequence
with goofball astonishment. But who's

ever ready for the animal call of the crazies?
I'd forgotten that the distance I'd built
between fear and the illusory calm,
the gap that kept shock at bay,
had left its edgy scar.

                By the time Brick
lifted Lily's shirt and bra to show us his name
filigreed in an ornate U beneath her nipple,
I'd long forsaken grass and chemicals.
Lily was two kids into her late thirties,
and its slight pendent swell
should have made me think her breast
exquisitely erotic. But the tattoo was so new
it raised her flesh in blistered relief
and the quick rush in my gut atomized.
Brick smiled and nodded, pinching
Lilly's blouse high, his thumb
and forefinger ever so lightly rubbing
the blond cotton fold back and forth.

      4.

The story in the magazine went something
like this: There are five of us jabbering
in slow motion under a wide old tree,
a joint circling in the kind of spring air
that laps your skin with profound affection.
Roots bulge softly like backrests.
There's only the present, a constant cycle
of astonishing insights. We're not hungry yet.
Just then a dog trots up, a dog in a bandana,
and he stops for petting, and we're laughing
at dogness itself, the happy panting,
the absurdist soul of dog! And soon enough
we're rolling on the grass, convulsing

in good cosmic hysteria.

                     Then, the sun rises.
A lot. The lunatic pulls the gun out
of the sky and sticks it down the back
of his pants and flaps his denim jacket
over it. The cross-legged swami
floats off with lizard cool
like a sheriff. The door he exits
closes in another realm. Someone marries
and heads for Europe, returns. There's four
of us, then six—hard to keep track. Finally,
Brick releases Lily's blouse. She feigns
a witty remark.

                 A decade of jobs, then
another reunion, the same tree calling to us.
Ralph pulls out a fresh joint and sends it
circling. Two tokes each. The afternoon
presses at the eardrums until the world
outside is a mean, echoing distance.
Two more tokes. A tightening
at the throat. Shadows spider.
Bushes shift like uniforms. No one
wants to lie on the ground. Ralph snaps
a clawed hand. A story trails off.
You hear every word you speak wobble
in a reverb. Only, you haven't spoken.
Then, a sideways glance, another,
as if each friend is a circus mirror.
Then, the worst nostalgia:
The skin of the body is a hide.
We're the joke. We've become the dog.

ELIZABETH AT SEABROOK

—nuclear power protests

I can re-imagine the turning face
Of that young guardsman irradiated
By dawn sun—or the fissured power plant.
He said, Ma'am, you know my orders: It's time
To separate the men from the women.
On the damp armory floor, the men sat
In circles, then the women around them.
At the center were piled our tied shoes.
We were surrounded by a tight square
Of masked soldiers holding shields, Billy clubs.
I stood to tell the lieutenant of our
Consensus pact: The instant a guardsman
Touches any one of our group, every
Man and woman will strip naked. Like that,
Rouge shadows blossomed on his cheeks the way
A thumb touch might shame any fresh petal
Into darkness. Their retreat took seconds.
Then we sat alone in the new silence.

One afternoon walk I'd seen a flower
Arranged in a Fibonacci sequence
Of new helical rays. What was its name?
The artist says beauty walks math spirals
Out past numbers, out past all reason.
That's a moment to live for, isn't it?
I had always believed that peace was won
Unarmed in the face of odds. —Who could know
Naked skin would send them into shadow.
They gave up and let us out. For two days
I slept and dreamed. At first the nuke sent up

A mushroom cloud. Then night, distant voices,
My mother, a ring of linked friends, moonlight.
I'm strolling through the wetlands, alone,
Wearing only my hiking boots. The sucking
Muck holds steps like kisses. Fibonacci
Florets billow in the sky. When I wake,
That flower's lost name burns me alive.

INQUIRY OF THE THE POETS' ASSEMBLY

—election night ghazal

Where are we going, Walt Whitman?
A map pixels the phone's screen.

Does ripe fruit never fall?
The brute mauls at his meats.

What to make of a diminished thing?
The dry tree sings in a fiery plume.

Where are the waters of childhood?
Not touchstones. Never the dream.

Ought I to regret my seedtime?
Ocean waters rot the street.

Must we dream our dreams and have them too?
The search convenes within a tossed room.

"…nothing? Do you remember 'Nothing'?"
A voice inside the voice inside these walls.

Of those so close behind me, which are you?
A question posed only to a blind mirror.

What shall flatter the desolate?
A smattering of faux applause.

What happens to a dream deferred?
Words interred in the gut with gall.

Are you our sort of person?
The courts grant no favor.

And what of the dead?
Figureheads, their petrified laws.

Then what was that rank flavor of blood?
My words, gleaned upon the mud bank—

REGS

Before unlocking the door, Derek likes staring in the portal window for a long time, watching Jack watching Jill as they huddle in their chairs near the giant monitor. They wear shirts in anticipation of his arrival.

Jack can't move but he speaks a language Jill gets. Jill speaks words in slow motion. She can move her arms. She points at the penis on the screen, jumping and falling, jumping and falling, the woman's hair something like wet.

Derek lifts Jack out of his Tracer SX and lays him down on the double bed. Jill grins with purpose as Derek removes Jack's long sleeve shirt. Jack's face and head are shaven. Only the front of Jack's face is without ink.

After college, I moved back home to Orange County. I didn't know what I wanted to do with my life. I'd been an English major, so I was thinking things through. I figured I'd call around for local work. Soon enough, I'm sending day nurses into the field. To hell with the regs, says my boss every time. Send Derek.

Derek knows I once followed him. He told me the drill never changes. Jill sends a laser into the pan of her Mariner chair. With deliberate ceremony, she takes off her shirt and bra. She has small formless legs, so soft that their white flesh holds the puncture of Derek's grip for minutes.

Everything I say here is true. Even the names. Against state regulations, Derek lifts Jill into the harness hung by a pulley above the bed. Its seat has three holes, two for her legs. Jack's erection points at the harness. I once told Derek, Listen, I didn't think they could get them. His eyes smiled as he shrugged.

Now Derek goes to the crank on the wall and lowers Jill down on Jack. Adjustments are necessary. Derek maneuvers the harness so Jack and Jill are one. Derek admitted he's disturbed by the way her alabaster legs—that's the word he always uses, *alabaster*—contrast with Jack's blue and red tattoos of underworld demons, human limbs dangling from their teeth.

Derek goes to the crank and turns the handle back and forth. It seems like a dream, he says. Sometimes slowly, sometimes fast. Jill no longer has to tell him. Jack doesn't make that gurgle. Derek can read their minds. I'm thinking things through. My boss doesn't want to know any more than he has to.

ON THE NEWS AS THIRD PROPHECY
OF THE TRUE BELIEF ANNOUNCED IN FIRE
ON THE FLORAL COAST

> The second woe is past, and behold,
> the third woe commeth quickly.
> —Revelations 11: 14

Waiting on line today, I met ol' Sam Flaherty,
pushing three-ten if a pound, his face a mirror,

his face a happy twin calling me from the other side,
his belt hung over a Walgreens cart of prescriptions

for god-knows-what, though he held one pill jar up
real quick, winked at me like a spy who'd decoded

just enough secrets in my notebook. We killed
time comparing new teeth. His face gleamed

in reflection. Nice fangs, he says…almost big
as the boar's fangs they pulled out of that guy down

Bonita Springs. Word was, the sucker was a second
amendment *dee-vo-taye*. If he didn't have the gun,

he wouldn't have a life. (Notation: liberty as breath.
Notation: freedom to carry.) Not that I need to carry,

one of us said, but every day I can feel rivulets
of flame spindling my blood. Don't mind

the burning air, it's like I'm running from myself.
Last year, word was meth factories hid backwoods

below Lee County pines, the cartel having trained
steroidal boars to snort themselves cross-county

strapped with panniers full of their fast magic.
I moved here from Jersey, where doubt is an accent,

but the idea of hauler boars seems monstrous likely
now. (Notation: boars in next letter to ed?) Sam

bends in to whisper—they found a twenty-kilo blend
of meth, coke, and love boat on the beast. I'd forgotten

how Sam practiced street talk like a man always got
an ankle holster fully loaded. Guys in Secaucus

would approve. No shit, I say. None, he nods.
Man, what do you think? I ask. Time we get

the state Guard come in and blow them tunnels?
Well—and now he yaws so low I can hardly hear—

word is, some rogue special ops are coming to do us
a solid, you know? But I didn't, just shifted my gut.

Sam's eyes near rolled outta his sockets. I can be slow
on the uptake was his body's meaning. He composed

himself, the line dead-stopped for some snowbird
whose prescription wouldn't ring up. I could see

myself coming for the going. Coulda been me
a few years back, a Yank without papers, waiting

to pay for my Z scrip. Now I'm Sam. Always
have been. Remember, he warns, you won't hear

the special ops copters until the downwash
coats you good. (Notation: downwash. Notation:

feel the air's flood.) They say the fuel's an aphrodisiac.
These guys…Lord God, no military permit, no

DC warrant, all prepped with bunker busters
you don't drop from the air. Two old farts on line

slip a look my way. What, like I shouldn't listen?
(Notation: become invisible?) I could tell Sam liked

the way my eyes must've gassed into big balloons.
He ignores the audience of shoppers humped along

the counter. Dark web, Jack. Dark web's the news,
he insists. They fix on a cave mouth, set the timers,

then let these night-vision snake-drones do their nasty.
Ten years I've been reading *War Tech Today*,

but I couldn't recall the snake bomb. (Notation:
Write editor, ask why no story. Notation:

Daniel 2.) Trouble is, Sam's complaining…
collateral damage. Might let 'em pussy out. What

do you mean? I ask, newly indignant. He mouths
real slow and silent like my father giving

righteous instruction out of mother's earshot:
Sex slaves…child porn…for-sale babies…

The tunnels, man, he breathes. It's off-shore Satanic
plague-shit down there. (Notation: Satanic. Notation:

plague. Notation: Revelations.) And the whole game
plan is run like Musso-friggin-lini, straight outta

the governor's office, too, that blue-faced south state
sumbitch. Runs a network from those so-called mom-

and-pop stores, ain't that pretty. Every lottery ticket
you buy from him is a GPS marker. Gimme your email,

Sam demands, I'll send you the link. I'm thinking,
Time is a lurch.

                    I'm alone mid-afternoon writing fast
in a faux New York pizza joint off Summerlin,

a light-sucking end-of-world storm cloud
shelling the place with marble-hard raindrops.

Just trying to hack up Sam's counsel, his words
like dream-ink drying into disappearance

on the page. (Notation: the page as revelation.)
A doughy slice coughs up its last oily bubble.

I think I feel like nodding, only who can afford
to sleep anymore? The guy behind the counter

had a beard ten minutes ago. I forget to think
about his face. In a jet stream second the cloud

blisters east, sun shafting my table through
the plate glass. When I look up, some guy

with my face, pulls an AR from a golf bag.
The gleaming.

                    It's true what they say, a soldier's
born prepared or not. The guy lifts the business end

skyward, blows a five-foot maw in the ceiling,
then stares in at me with raging compassion,

like I'm a member of the tribe. Mouth still
as a mannequin, his words echoing from the wall

speakers in a déjà vu reverb. The holy fire
is at hand, Jack. (Notation: Knows my name,

change passwords?) The lord is riding down
the flames on a night-black boar, says his head

in my head. My children *shall* be saved.
Leave, he warns, if you believe this page

shall become as blood. (Notation: _____.)
The man's eyes lit as sanction. Can you feel

my pulse? Can you smell the fuel? Sirens
announce my heart. There's his world, then

mine. Gun as purifying flame. Finger palsied
on the trigger. I write to you from inside

the beast—
           such beauty I cannot forsake...

—November 8, 2016

THREE

I WANT TO SEE

The gutted and the crushed returning
To life right now, their ascension
Into good flesh. I want to see
Photosynthetic joy burning
From the center of ten-thousand leaves,
Moist earth turned over and over
By unseeable animalia. I want

The distant refugees and the political
Prisoners and the trafficked, all
Past hope of crying, and the near
Friends, unconscious and rushed
To emergency rooms— I want them all
To come home tonight while the table
Is set and the sun slants upon the bowls.

But I'm told all of my yearning is foolish,
Forget what you want. Forget the ghosts,
Forget the slain and soon-to-be. Forget
The long odds. I'm told to forget the gods
Cocooned in their silence, to forget
The best intentions and the worst. Think
Instead of the bowls sunning on the table.

And, for the sake of this breath this light
This meal this touch these words, I do.

HONEYMOON GATORS

—1949

Catholic as sin, sure of the *mysterium fidei*, my parents
rarely questioned the edicts, nor
how soul meets
flesh. I was conceived in their postwar version
of love,
a sunburnt motel near the St. Augustine Alligator Farm,

rope bridges dangling above tooth and tail. Later,
her sighs, smirks, half-heard asides
drifting unresolved
into funereal afternoons implied
a splintering,
a harrowing of their bed, the very private

failures of the bodies of Christ.
Once, long after he died, she admitted she couldn't
fathom why
he'd brought her to that place:
When one of those beasts pried open a long yawn,
I felt I'd fallen

into its gape. As a child awash in the Lenten incense
of Good Friday mass, I stared
in perplexed wonder at the smoke-
shadowed stained glass, just as I stared every night
at the pitch-
black ceiling above my bed, higher

than the agonistic crucifix nailed to the wall.
Their handsome bloodied God

demanded fidelity
as much to an hermetic plan as to each other,
the sacramental
distilments of sex and station. Once

I heard my father laugh, then swear at his heroic nemesis
Cardinal Spellman who spoke from TV
in a plummeting gravity
of voice, as if sin
must be met by an equal ruin.
I turned from my mother at the Sunday stove, her head nodding

in silence. Those nights, afloat in lightlessness, filling not
with Jesus
but the stuff of lordly eclipse, I sensed how
the unlit absence
between the plastic glowing stars
that my father in his love for me had pressed above my bed

held the *mysterium secularum* of my origin. I was twelve
before he broached the facts of the flesh
once and once
only. Now after the great indulgence
of god-free marriage,
I often wake upon entering an aperture

in the ceiling, drift beyond god and the godless
theorems, forsaking
the hard-earned absolutes
of unbelief, alert
instead to the sub-atomic percolations, a new set
of doctrines, all intimating

a wide road where a quantum string music
answers the fields,
granting me free, if
mortal, purpose. And once more I'm there
with my parents, compelled
as they are by an as yet indiscernible

pulse. See? We're all timed and timeless, which is why
they're forever
turning their nuptial DeSoto
north for the blessed first apartment, each alone
with their Word, squinting
in the ravenous windshield maw of the Florida sun.

TGA

> During *transient global amnesia*, your recall of recent events
> simply vanishes, so you can't remember where you are or how
> you got there. Episodes always improve gradually over a few hours.
> —Mayo Clinic

Then, after a six-decade snap of my life's breath,
I'm simply walking, lost
in the unwitting fakery
of selfhood,
down a hallway that should be tread-deep familiar, the wall

frames, the tufted carpet— But whose
alien sense
is this, from where
does this forgetting erupt, what year is it? The neurologist keeps
strobing over me, there,

not
there. He checks again—and I'm answering with the wrong president,
the wrong date, the present
dispersing the past
into an amnesiac burst of lost atoms. Sixty years earlier

my father slumbered in a waiting room, walled off
from my mother's birthing
howls, Harry Caray
on the hospital's scratchy stand-up GE calling 1950's last
spring-training game,

a foreign air
that same moment invading what had been my dark
boundless world,

an untouchable blaze of light, my ascendance in the doctor's
cold womb-

sized hands
up
into something other, an icy warmth flooding beneath the skin,
a *not-me* so blue
then spark-white, the first break

incessant and without sense. What
could my father and I
expect
from the start but some version of any story, the sourceless
dirt road

splaying happenstance into ten-thousand tributaries,
only one of which we follow
with intent?
Harry's long
dead. My father, too. And yet, as prophetic as The Babe,

the doc's next question unlocks one dearly fixed memory
—my father and I leaning
before dinner
over
a tiny Lafayette transistor, Opening Day rushing toward us,

the Cardinals rife with hard lumber and oiled leather,
my questions answered
in the speculative
anticipatory lilt
of his love, the same love I've carried to this brink,

how he punctuates
each guy's chances
as Harry intones the batting order— That's when I hear
an old voice
in my mouth

announcing by God the entire lineup
of so many
decades previous— And that smiling baseball doc
promises, No worries,
you'll be born

in short order back into your old self. —As if all along
he'd thought it was merely my own voice
called up
from the ceaseless birthright shock
of beginning.

POSTMODERN NIGHTS

—The Capay Valley, CA

You'd think the stars were emissaries,
the way I'd still my pulse to listen on the floor
of the razed barn, ardent for signals.
Was it love or the click of fate that sent

my wife out to search with me? Neither the stars
nor the mammal folds of the coastal range—
dimly lit by a waning crescent—would sing
testimonials to a universe I'd been taught

by theory to drain of breath. I'd press myself
behind her and breathe the simple atoms of scent
from her hair. Soon, eyes closed, I'd slide my arms
across her breasts. She'd push her whole body

back into me. And so, I'd hold to the real, pulsars
flashing their beams against the absent light.

THE CONSECRATIONS

We can imagine the long gray muscle trolling
off San Simeon, circling the guano-slick rock, we
can imagine the unconscious, the epochs, rock

disintegrating in silt-grained increments, we
can imagine instinct, its depth, the beast a ripped
slither in the subsurface predawn gray, the slash

of electrodes suddenly firing, the dopaminic bliss
of the ancient trance, and again the circling,
then uncurling fifty miles north until, in a single

flexed shiver, it breaks south the same second
we wake to kiss and rise, synched in the usual
dream state lean for morning air, soon to assure

each other the water the asphalt the coast morning...
that these are the consecrations, the communion,
how we'll meet at beachside, her kiss, her teeth

pricking my lip in a last tug through the car window
before she leaves to swim her ocean mile,
the promise to meet for coffee at shoreline—

and soon she's yanked up the back strap of her wetsuit,
presses the goggles to her face as the waves wrap
her legs, the same moment my right foot clicks both

cleats into pedals as the hill pulls my bike in a glide path
down Pacific, where Sunday's devout float from Grace
Church without a nod my way, where the hump-backed

at Sunshine Donuts in their re-caffeinated seclusion
scratch silver paste from cards as I circuit past, all
the neurons of the saved and lonely funneled into

the blindered present, each waiting for the holy
number to come up, while out here the unknown
unfolds on face and hands, a blessing through which

her arms pull in a metric churn, my own shoulders
in first ache, my legs gone lactic from climbing
up-valley before the free fall purge of the no-hands

descent down Squire Canyon to the hard left onto
Monte Road—a cleansing but for the old man
firing a pistol into the waist-high mustard, then

the low riot of wild turkey bursting through
my front wheel, an instant resolve to outlast
the forward fall, then the roll, helmet split on asphalt,

the decapitated head of turkey rolling behind me,
road burn a strawberried smear across my right side,
one spoke snapped, but the bike an intact miracle,

scraped but uncracked, and so I unbend myself
into a crackling stand, how I can't yet know that
five hundred yards offshore she catches sight

of the dark-blur long form a body's length beneath,
the lung-deep charge to bolt, while here the bent man's
face curdles into confusion, his limbs shaken by guilt

as I fight the air-stung scald into cooling, and,
as if it's my job to pull him back from the edge
of seizure, I raise my hand to him so he'll see

I'm unbroken, then bear my good leg over the cross-
bar, and press the pedals into the old promise,
the man shrinking wordless behind me, just as my wife

stops mid-stroke, kicks both legs before her, a savage
last-chance will to take on the inevitable jaws, how
she waits on the calm sea—she tells me later—when,

finally, three yards off in a sleek burbled upsurge
of ocean: a sea lion breaks the surface to stare at her
with glib disdain, how she swore at the harmless beast,

her breath choked in last fear as I clutch her now,
the children of tourists splashing farther into the surf,
the ocean's mouth muscling open for communion.

IN BETWEEN

I'd always told myself
the late night moonlight
glow riding her skin as
she slept was a matter
of pure matter, simple
science. The way the world
builds itself. I believed her
low blaze to be atomic
deceit, particles arranged
to dupe me back into
an abiding realm where
the question is written
as a rhetorical answer—
a shimmering borealis
claiming true north.
But then she'd lift
from the bottom layer
of a dream to pull my face
toward her, squinting
at some nether version
of the fool she knew
she'd married for love—
and I'd try to sleep.

One midnight the farmhouse
we rented dead center
of the almond orchard
shook in moonless wind
as if to dare me into
the dark. And it did—
I left our bed, stepping
soundlessly onto

the peeling porch,
then upon the patch
of night-black grass, and
stood as still as the wind
would allow. I could hear
in the infinite webs
of almond limbs a high
voice I knew was no
voice, but, rather, a siren
risen from ancient ganglia,
the sound of a whistling
taunt, a tinnitus
betraying my belief
in only the tactile. And
even if it were nothing
more than high-pitched
worry sending me back
to her side all aching
night, I held out
my hand, tried to gauge
the untouchable
hovering from her—

AMPLITUDE

We're talking a party with good friends
when in the dark hallway one leans
over my wife, *his* wife laughing
in another room, purrs how he'd
take her upstairs right now,
she'd never regret it—*nor*, he adds,
any other day she'd care to meet,
his hand with clichéd timing
stretched for a phantom strand
of her hair. —Should I be done

with thinking it through? When
I bake a thought past burnt,
she likes to remind me how
we're so empty that neutrinos
from distant nebulae sail through us
without collision. Given such
amplitude, what swinish offense
should matter today? But a primal
insistence flares: Maybe I'd been out

of town, maybe I was playing ball.
Years back my shock would arc forth
upon hearing the few other times
when men had thrown their futile
Hail Mary's her way, so she knows
too well my adrenal blurts. You'd think
I wandered the Darwinian plain,
hormonal poles skewing
the compass. You'd think I was

fifteen, urgent and dreamy: How
we all ached for Hal's mother,
our romantic burn soon burnished
into more than teen swoon
when Hal's father blew out
his heart in a pick-up game
of CYO hoops. After the funeral,
a kind of breathy song pearled
our voices each time we asked Hal
why she wore black everywhere
she went for a year. She'd nod to us,
rarely speak. Later we'd head
to the recesses of our rooms, new
moon shadows waving imperceptibly
upon bed sheets. How we'd find
our sight setting crosstown
on another darkening room, imbued
by god with the scent of want. Flash
forward, home from college, the five
of us at Hal's house screaming
at the game when, like fine mist
twirled into the impalpable,
a white dress with gold brocade
floats past the corner of our eyes.
The game nulls into white noise.
When the doorbell rings, we spin
to see chalk-haired, owl-eyed
Mr. Oxford, the town vet, his head
like a giant pumpkin, his eyes
thickly threaded blood-red under
gold specs. Hell if memory
doesn't serve up so many shades

of shame. Sure, even then we knew
our deflation was Freudian.
In the years of comic retelling
that followed, we each witnessed
their ungainly exit out the door
into god-please-help-us a date.
How we'd cheated ourselves
into such vast distances, girls
breeze-blown atop a mountain
while we squinted at them from
our walled village. I always want

the story to be about the Judas friend
who crossed into piggery.
It does no good to reimagine
his hand lifting the missing strand
of my wife's hair as he leaned
up close. And to think of the foolish pride
that swirled in the vortex of my chest.
It wasn't only how she'd foiled him
with deflective charm—so light-speed
smart—pearl-necklace-under-flannel
grace—but rather the fact of other men
drawn to her. How one's love might
percolate all that saltier when recalling
the obvious. Have you ever stepped

onto a balcony to find yourself
surveying a formal gathering,
say, a fundraiser
for an indisputable cause?
And then, Look—over there:
Do you see those laughing men
circled in thrall around one woman,

her off-the-shoulder tea-dance gown,
the shining sea-blue taffeta
slowly spiraling back and forth?
What joke has she quipped in faux rue?
How many seconds before you realize
her swirling aquamarine gesture
formed a tropical inlet into which
you'd been swimming only hours ago?
When she angles away from the group
to rotate her view, she seems
to be searching the room. All
the colors no human can see
traverse you now
like unanswerable questions. —So
yes, this is the moment that matters:
The long free fall before you lean
over the rail to wave, then wait out
the perpetual instant,
willing the particles of her gaze
into the spinning vortex of your own.

MATERIALIST NOIR

Love must ride a weak carrier wave here
In the land of just the facts, m'am. Let me
Promise— The post-coital scent of your hair,
Your dreams in code, your eyes steeped clear as tea,

The white heroin of your inner thigh…
I've hidden each essential gift in rooms
Far from those detectives who have to try
All evidence for unimpeachable proof

Of absolute zero. —And I should know,
I'm one of them questioning two selves: Dead
Sure and Maybe Not. When you radio
Me from behind your book, from deep in bed,

From the patio dahlias, there's no place
The cops find us. We're gone without a trace.

FOUR

THE DRIVER

I'd hitchhiked out of Atlanta, smoked
a joint with two guitarists, amped
stories strung out like rock ballads
while we rattled the speed limit.
What's likely? Not a blue sedan

easing onto the margin ahead—
I figured the driver
had stopped to check a map, so I jumped
from the van, threw on
my pack, then threw out
my thumb to catch a ride onto 75,
only to hear the horn, an apparitional hand
out the window waving me
forward. You think I'm committing
fantasy, but when I leaned

into the passenger window, her face
kaleidoscoped like the fifth dimension
of a pop-up book. I'd saved one
from childhood, all these perfect little trees
along the calmest stretch
of empty road, the next pages flipping
into gifts as the road ribboned through portraits
of paradisal farms, a girl's blonde hair
lilting without affect
in the kind of breeze so comforting
that when we let down our guard of facts
we'd come to call it predestined.

Those days we were all of us open
to the kind of drug-lit synchronicities

full of inexplicable sense. I was an atheist,
God a jokester with a kind heart.

I'm heading to Gainesville.
I know, she said.

By then, acid had taken me
across the line more than once.
Nothing to trust, just the thrill
of wide gaps
in the rules we played by. There was the midnight
Ralph and I seemed to swim
through rocks of air
beneath bulbous bags of primary colors,
large oval gobbets
hung by pranksters from trees in a copse.
For hours we tested echoes. Your voice
never plays the same after globes
drip themselves from the stars. Last month

on a call Ralph recounted that night
with the kind of sentiment reserved
for events that can hardly bear up
under language. Twice we had to ask,
Had it been the acid? Or...? —Nothing
else happened. We'd both wanted
all the secrets
to reveal themselves. Or so we thought.
But wasn't it the next secret,
the one behind disclosure,
that drew us further
up into the altitudes? How could the driver

know where I was heading? By Macon
the talk was ascendant, tires
choralling above the four-lane,
"Astral Weeks" soundtracking
on the stereo. She'd foreknown
we were pulling over, that I'd be in need
of a lift, the drive

a life apart. In the accelerant
language of converts,
we described the uncanny—
my father's story of an ex-girlfriend's letter
arriving in futile desire
the same day he and my mother walked out
on a bridge and tossed
their diaphragm into the current
of hopes. The driver's thoughts
spiraled like incense
through my own. I played
my doubt like dice as winnings
tacked with each toss.

She said she'd died once, then rose
over herself, looking down
upon her body on the coagulating asphalt
as the EMTs scrambled
their gear upon her chest and mouth.
She shook her head at the view
of incomprehensible beauty
fountaining up from the scene, her own body.
Before I could ask, she declared herself
unready, and so in a perfect dive
she sent her soul sweeping down
into the chalice

of her heart as the little monitor
came beeping back to life.

Miles sped through the windshield,
the driver and I infused
with the incorporeal music
of voices passing
through us. Look, we called. The car nosed
between rows of see-through bodies,
floating in ghostly sleep,
long parallel cues of the soon-to-be
sliding on invisible chutes into…what? we didn't know—

When we parted at my exit, her hand
out the window rode
the jet stream goodbye. Across town
in my bed the sleeping body
of a girl who'd soon leave me.

                    *

Last month I left the house for a lactic-fast bike ride
while the afternoon calmed the seasonal winds
and the heat pulsed up
from the road. Returning,
I set the bike in the garage and stepped
into a home I barely remembered.
Had the odds shifted?

My son looked up from his desk, followed me
down the hall. Was he asking
an unanswerable question?

Twelve hours later I was waking
in a room off the ER. The neurologist nods,
says "transient global amnesia" means
you'll be back in a few hours' time.
I couldn't recall the date, or the president
for that matter. But I can tell you this:

Through those hours of transit,
you hover just out of reach,
as if you're in a transparent bowl
you can't see from. And there's
that sound, a soft blue song
sung through you. —But the words, the lyrics…
When you get back, they're impossible
to grasp, motes of dust
                    floating on the other side—

NOTES

Elegy:
Angels with Dirty Faces (Warner Brothers, 1938).

The Calling:
Some congregations of Catholic nuns have adhered to a theology in which they marry Jesus.

Dog:
"Windowpane" is a type of LSD soaked in small pieces of paper. "Gold" is short for "Acapulco Gold," a strain of mythically powerful marijuana.
"White crosses" are amphetamine pills.

Elizabeth at Seabrook:
In 1977, demonstrators temporarily shut down the construction of the Seabrook, N.H., nuclear power plant. Practicing non-violence, they were arrested and placed in an armory. When the jailers announced that the men and women were to be split up, the counterplan described in the poem was devised—most likely by Elizabeth Boardman, a Quaker. The jailers withdrew their order and retreated. Over time, the protestors were released, and charges were dropped.

The Fibonacci sequence is a mathematical progression that often mirrors biological arrangements such as the flowering of an artichoke.

Inquiry of the Poets' Assembly:
Source poems of italicized lines:
Alan Ginsberg, "A Supermarket in California"
Wallace Stevens, "Sunday Morning"
Robert Frost, "Oven-Bird"
Mark Strand, "Where Are the Waters of Childhood?"
Robert Lowell, "Memories of West Street and Lepke"
Elizabeth Bishop, "Questions of Travel"
T.S. Eliot, "The Waste Land"
Theodore Roethke, "The Waking"

Gwendolyn Brooks, "The Lovers of the Poor"
Langston Hughes, "Harlem"
Sylvia Plath, "The Applicant"
Anne Sexton, "The Truth the Dead Know"
Galway Kinnell, "The Bear"

On the News as Third Prophecy of the True Belief Announced in Fire on the Floral Coast:

Throughout the latter stages of the 2016 presidential election, paranoid conspiracies about Hilary Clinton included the bizarre assertion that she and her campaign were running a child sex ring from the back of a particular pizza restaurant in Washington D.C. Though the setting is switched to Florida, the poem is inspired by an event that took place a month after the election in which a man entered the restaurant and fired a weapon while trying to find the phantom children and perpetrators. "Love Boat" is the mind-altering drug "angel dust."

Honeymoon Gators:

The Latin term *mysterium fidei* translates to "mystery of faith," an idiom that dates back to Catholic theological circles in the 1500s.

"String Theory" proposes that the universe is comprised of one-dimensional "strings" rather than individual particles. Some quantum physicists contend that string theory helps to explain how the universe functions simultaneously on the atomic and subatomic levels.

The Driver:

"Astral Weeks" is the title song of an album by Van Morrison (Warner Brothers Records, 1968).

ACKNOWLEDGMENTS

Thanks to the editors of the following magazines and anthologies for publishing these poems, some in slightly different form and/or with different titles:

American Journal of Poetry — "The Shapes at Quechee"
Arroyo Literary Review — "Dog"
Askew — "Materialist Noir"
Chicago Quarterly Review — "The Calling"
Community College Humanities Review — "On the News as Third Prophecy of the True Belief Announced in Fire on the Floral Coast"; "Postmodern Nights"
Epoch — "The Consecrations"
The Georgia Review — "Two Stories"
Gulf Coast — "Regs"
Hotel Amerika — "Conceit"; "Museum of the Morning After"
Lake Effect — "Amplitude"
The Packinghouse Review — "Before Dinner"
Poetry Northwest — "In Between"
Prairie Schooner — "Hank's Choice"; "The Oscillations"
Rattle — "Elegy"
Salt — "I Want to See"; "The Driver"
The Southern Review — "Admitting Belief"
Weber — "Inquiry of the Poets' Assembly"

A Face to Meet the Faces: An Anthology of Contemporary Persona Poetry — "Elizabeth at Seabrook"

Love Rise Up: An Anthology of Social Justice, Protest and Hope — "Elizabeth at Seabrook"

I'm forever gratified by the generous assistance of so many people. At the Bolinas Salon: Wendy Barker and Hannah Stein. In San Luis Obispo: Ginger Adcock, John Hampsey, Mary Kay Harrington, Al Landwehr, and Todd James Pierce; Michele Flom and Sarah Grieve; Lisa Coffman and Mira Rosenthal. In Port Townsend: Stan Sanvel Rubin. In the wide world: Ralph Black, Brad Comann, Stephen Corey, Greg Glazner, Lauren Henley, Jonathan Maule, and Jim Reese. Memorial thanks to Adam Hill, Judith Kitchen, and Brandon Kershner, whose works live on as art, idea, and influence. Thanks to Sara Henning and Kimberly Verhines at Stephen F. Austin State University Press for their wisdom and editorial know-how. Thanks as well to my students everywhere from whom I continue to learn. I'm grateful too for the support of Rick Barot and my colleagues at the Rainier Writing Workshop in Tacoma. My thanks to photographer Dennis Steers for his author photo and to artist Elaine Spatz-Rabinowitz for use of her painting *Amaryllis*. Particular thanks to the brilliant poets whose endorsements appear on the book's cover. Special thanks to my aunt, Mary Higgins Clark (1927-2020), whose genial lifelong encouragement continues to help me uncover the next line. And most profound thanks to my wife Amy Hewes for a lifetime of first and subsequent readings; you sustain me.

ABOUT THE AUTHOR

Kevin Clark teaches at The Rainier Writing Workshop. *The Consecrations* is his third full-length volume of poems. His second book *Self-Portrait with Expletives* won the Pleiades Press prize. His first collection *In the Evening of No Warning* earned a grant from the Academy of American Poets. His most recent chapbook *The Wanting* won the Five Oaks Press contest. Kevin's poems appear in the *Southern, Georgia, Iowa,* and *Antioch* reviews, as well as *Crazyhorse, Ploughshares, Prairie Schooner, Poetry Northwest, Gulf Coast,* etc. His poetry is anthologized in several volumes, including *Keener Sounds: Selected Poems from The Georgia Review* and *The Notre Dame Review: The First Ten Years.* He is *The Literary Review*'s Angoff Award winner and the inaugural selectee for the ArtSmith Award. Kevin has published essays in *The Georgia Review, The Iowa Review, The Southern Review,* and *Contemporary Literary Criticism.* The poet laureate of San Luis Obispo County (CA), he is the author of *The Mind's Eye,* a poetry-writing textbook from Pearson Longman.

His website is: http://kevinclarkpoetry.com.

CPSIA information can be obtained
at www.ICGtesting.com
Printed in the USA
FSHW011136221021
85651FS